This Is the Ocean
Hardcover first edition • August 2025 • ISBN: 978-1-958629-88-8
eBook first edition • August 2025 • ISBN: 978-1-958629-90-1
Paperback coming soon.

Written by Elizabeth Everett, Text © 2025
Illustrated by Evelline Andrya, Illustrations © 2025

Project Manager, Cover and Book Design: Skyler Kaczmarczyk, Washington, D.C.
Editors: Hannah Thelen, Washington, D.C.
         Violet Antonick, Washington, D.C.
Editorial Assistants: Gweneth Kozlowski, Sudeeksha Dasari, and Daryn Schvimmer

Bilingual reversible edition (EN/SP) • November 2025 • ISBN: 978-1-958629-95-6

Teacher's Guide available at the Educational Resources page of ScienceNaturally.com.

Published in the United States by:
Science, Naturally! - An imprint of Platypus Media, LLC
1140 3rd Street NE
Suite 200
Washington, DC 20002
(202) 546-1674
Info@ScienceNaturally.com • ScienceNaturally.com

Distributed to the book trade by:
Baker & Taylor Publisher Services (North America)
Toll-free: (888) 814-0208
Orders@btpubservices.com • Btpubservices.com

Library of Congress Control Number: 2024952169

10 9 8 7 6 5 4 3 2 1

Schools, libraries, government, and non-profit organizations can receive bulk discounts.
Contact us at the address above or email us at Info@ScienceNaturally.com for more information.

The front cover may be reproduced freely, without modification, for review or non-commercial educational purposes.

All rights reserved. No part of this book may be reproduced in any form without the express written permission of the publisher. Front cover exempted (see above).

Printed in China.

This Is the Ocean

Written by **Elizabeth Everett**
Illustrated by **Evelline Andrya**

Science, Naturally!
An imprint of Platypus Media, LLC

This is the **ocean**.

These are the **salty waves** that roll to and from the ocean.

This is the **light of the Sun**
that shines on the salty waves
that roll to and from the ocean.

This is the tiny **plankton** that makes its own food from the light of the Sun

that shines on the salty waves
that roll to and from the ocean.

This is the **krill** that swarms the surface to eat the plankton

that makes its own food from the light of the Sun
that shines on the salty waves
that roll to and from the ocean.

This is the **fish** that swims in a school to swallow the krill

that swarms the surface to eat the plankton
that makes its own food from the light of the Sun
that shines on the salty waves
that roll to and from the ocean.

This is the **crab** that swipes its claw to snatch the fish

that swims in a school to swallow the krill
that swarms the surface to eat the plankton
that makes its own food from the light of the Sun
that shines on the salty waves
that roll to and from the ocean.

This is the **octopus** that uses camouflage to trick the crab

that swipes its claw to snatch the fish
that swims in a school to swallow the krill
that swarms the surface to eat the plankton
that makes its own food from the light of the Sun
that shines on the salty waves
that roll to and from the ocean.

This is the **seal** that patiently searches to spot the octopus

that uses camouflage to trick the crab
that swipes its claw to snatch the fish
that swims in a school to swallow the krill
that swarms the surface to eat the plankton
that makes its own food from the light of the Sun
that shines on the salty waves
that roll to and from the ocean.

This is the **shark** that secretly stalks to chomp the seal

that patiently searches to spot the octopus
that uses camouflage to trick the crab
that swipes its claw to snatch the fish
that swims in a school to swallow the krill
that swarms the surface to eat the plankton
that makes its own food from the light of the Sun
that shines on the salty waves
that roll to and from the ocean.

This is the **whale** way down deep that swims in circles to strike the shark

that secretly stalks to chomp the seal
that patiently searches to spot the octopus
that uses camouflage to trick the crab
that swipes its claw to snatch the fish
that swims in a school to swallow the krill
that swarms the surface to eat the plankton
that makes its own food from the light of the Sun
that shines on the salty waves
that roll to and from the ocean.

This is the **plume** that floats in the water behind the whale

that swims in circles to strike the shark
that patiently searches to spot the octopus
that uses camouflage to trick the crab
that swipes its claw to snatch the fish
that swims in a school to swallow the krill
that swarms the surface to eat the plankton
that makes its own food from the light of the Sun
that shines on the salty waves
that roll to and from the ocean.

These are the tiny **plankton** that use the plume to grow...

and this is the **ocean** that brings the circle to life.

Meet the Author and Illustrator

Elizabeth Everett is an award-winning author of several STEM books for kids, including the *Skytime* series and *Spheres All Year*. As a former educator and a homeschooling mom, she loves creating books for kids that engage the heart and mind. Elizabeth currently lives in Boulder County, Colorado with her family in the foothills of the Rocky Mountains. In this companion book to *This Is the Sun*, she takes readers on an adventure through the ocean, helping them understand how the Sun impacts life below the waves. She can be reached at Elizabeth.Everett@ScienceNaturally.com.

For Darnell and Jalen
—E. E.

Evelline Andrya was born in Sumatra to a Chinese-Javanese family. Growing up in Indonesia, a country of 17,000 islands, she was immersed in a rich blend of cultures—colorful tribes, lush rainforests, diverse wildlife, an underwater paradise, and historical marvels—that became her inspiration for her vibrant artworks. Evelline is currently living in Java, Indonesia with her husband, their four children, and a fluffy Pomeranian. Find her on Instagram @evellineandrya.

For my family, my ocean of hope
—E. A.